WANDERLUST
Portland
A Creative Guide to the City

BETSY BEIER

WEST
MARGIN
PRESS

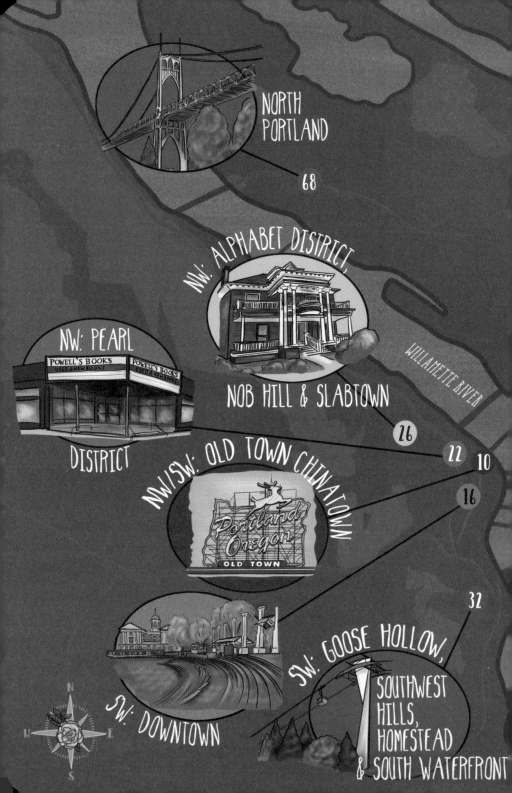

NORTH PORTLAND 68

NW: ALPHABET DISTRICT,

NW: PEARL

POWELL'S BOOKS
USED & NEW BOOKS

POWELL'S BOOKS
USED & NEW BOOKS

DISTRICT

NOB HILL & SLABTOWN

WILLAMETTE RIVER

26

22   10

NW/SW: OLD TOWN CHINATOWN

16

Portland
Oregon
OLD TOWN

32

SW: GOOSE HOLLOW,

SW: DOWNTOWN

SOUTHWEST
HILLS,
HOMESTEAD
& SOUTH WATERFRONT

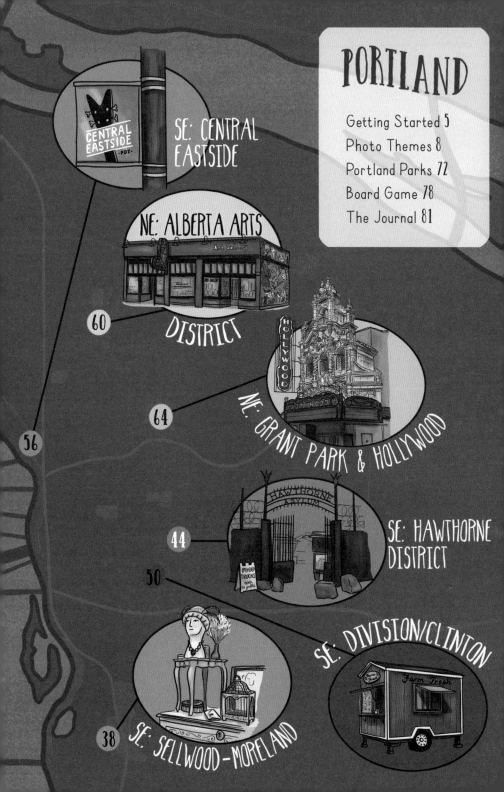

SE: CENTRAL EASTSIDE

NE: ALBERTA ARTS DISTRICT

NE: GRANT PARK & HOLLYWOOD

SE: HAWTHORNE DISTRICT

SE: DIVISION/CLINTON

SE: SELLWOOD-MORELAND

PORTLAND

56

60

64

44

50

38

INTRODUCTION

Located at the confluence of the Willamette and Columbia Rivers and surrounded by lush forests and stunning mountains is the outdoorsy, creative, and quirky city of Portland, Oregon. Divided by its residents into six "quadrants," Portland is a town of rugged individualism sprinkled with weirdness. It commends uniqueness and praises all types of entrepreneurs and creators, yet also has a strong commitment to community. The city embraces its industrial past, while also promoting progressive environmental ideas and sustainable practices. Portland exudes a strong sense of place that can be seen from its renowned food scene to its passionate maker culture. If there is ever a town that is made to be explored creatively, Portland is the place.

I'm a huge believer in experiential travel. When I visit a new location, I like to slow down long enough to be able to capture a sliver of what life might be like to live there. Of course I'll go see the top destinations a city might have to offer, but for me it's about making time to sit at a local cafe for an afternoon and soak up the vibe, or exploring a lesser-known neighborhood and watch people going about their day. It might be simply capturing the colors I see around the place, or making note of the slang words I hear from the locals in conversation.

Experiential travel is also about context, opening your eyes to learn a little about the history of the place while removing any preconceived judgements. Ultimately, it's about being open to any experience that may come your way.

So, join me on this creative journey as we explore the incredible city of Portland!

GETTING STARTED

Congratulations on deciding to explore Portland through a creative lens with this Wanderlust Guide! Grab a pen, a few color pencils, your phone, and this book, and you are set to go. Here are some pointers on getting started.

EXPLORE THE SIGHTS This book can be used as a travel guide before you head off on your journey or while you are actually at a location and looking around. Most chapters are about a specific neighborhood and some are citywide. Within each chapter, there is some high-level history, plus interesting facts and stories to give you a taste of the area. Just use the map on page 2 to look up the destination you are interested in exploring and head out the door!

JOURNAL & SKETCH YOUR EXPERIENCE I cherish the travel journals I have kept on my trips. Some are filled with watercolor scenes of our explorations, and others are just scribbled diaries of what we did that day. For me, a travel journal is not supposed to be perfect. It's an organic document of memories and stories while in a location. There's space throughout this book to write just the facts, and room to embellish your feelings and memories of the day.

PHOTO OP
Don't miss these photo opportunities! Look for this symbol throughout the book to find nearby sights for that perfect snapshot.

GET CREATIVE This book is all about getting creative and engaging in the local area you are exploring to have a unique and memorable experience. So if you have an inspiring idea, go for it! Some chapters provide artsy projects, some interactive games, while others encourage you to have fun with creative writing. The activities are meant to be spontaneous and entertaining. But you could also save the book activities until later in the day, perhaps at a cafe, or back at the hotel as you relive your adventures.

Now, it's time to get exploring!

ART SUPPLIES

I've learned over time that for packing art supplies, fewer is always better. A few black pens, a travel watercolor set, and a couple colored pencils are typically all I need. Occasionally, I'll bring along a glue stick or tape to add a unique wrapper, ticket stub, or scrap of paper I may find to my journal. You'll find plenty of room in the diary section for all these artistic and creative endeavors and any others you may think up!

THE GUIDE

PHOTO THEMES

A photo theme is a great way to see things you may not initially notice when touring a new spot. It's like a scavenger hunt to help you look beyond the sights and uncover the patterns and unique personality of a city. All you need is your phone and a theme—a color, an object, a style, an animal, etc. As you tour the city, hunt for your theme and snap a photo when you see it. By the end of the day, you may have taken ten pictures or hundreds of them.

   Once you've taken all these fabulous pictures, you can make DIY souvenir gifts for yourself! Create an art collage using a multi-photo frame, or put it all together in an artsy photo book. Here are some possible photo themes you can use.

SHADES OF GREEN

From the pine trees in Forest Park to the abundance of leafy vegetables at the Portland Farmers Market, there is no shortage of green to be found in Portland. Snap pictures of all the green things you find while you explore each neighborhood: a passerby's cool hoodie, a couch in a hotel lobby, a vintage lamp at a thrift shop, a mural on the side of a building, even a "Keep Green" environmental sticker. At the end of your visit, you will understand why Portland is considered a green city!

ROSES

There is a reason one of Portland's nicknames is the City of Roses—roses are everywhere! From the International Rose Test Garden to the rose gardens in Ladd's Addition, the city has celebrated this fragrant flower for over a century. While out and about, photograph as many roses as you see. When you return home, collage them together to create your very own bouquet.

BIKES

With miles of bike lanes, bike routes, bike-sharing programs, and even bicycle parking at the airport, Portland is a biker's paradise. Look for bicycle signs, bike paraphernalia, biking clothing and accessories, or wildly colored bikes. And if you are so inclined, rent a bike and record a video from your own eyes of biking around the city!

ZOOBOMB

Beginning in 2002 and still happening today, on Sunday nights a group of riders gather at the top of Washington Park with bikes of all types and race down the hill toward downtown. There is even a sculpture at West Burnside Street and SW 13th Avenue that sports a pile of bikes, called the Zoobomb Pyle. The sculpture not only pays tribute to the tradition but also provides a sort of bike lending system for those who want to participate in the Zoobomb ride but don't have a bike.

BRIDGES

Look around and you'll see why Portland is also called Bridge City and Bridgetown. Some bridges are dedicated to trains (Burlington Northern Railroad Bridge) while others are busy interstates (Marquam Bridge). Some move up and down for boats (Steel Bridge), and others open in the middle (Burnside Bridge). Some are very new (Tilikum Crossing Bridge), and some are over a century old (Hawthorne Bridge). Capture the bridges with your camera and collage the shots to reveal the true Bridgetown.

NW/SW: OLD TOWN CHINATOWN

Old Town Chinatown, the original downtown, has weathered its share of ups and downs. From the first landing spot of the Western pioneers to Willamette River floods, from debauchery and crime to trendy doughnuts and a makers' market, the area's colorful history provides a greater understanding of the culture of Portland itself!

The White Stag sign is at 70 NW Couch Street.

THE CLEARING

For thousands of years Chinookan peoples used the fertile land at the confluence of the Willamette and Columbia Rivers as a prime location for gathering food. Called "The Clearing" by early expeditioners, this was the location Lewis and Clark found during their famous expedition west in 1803–1806. From their praise came fur traders, missionaries, and others, bringing the Indigenous People prosperity but also diseases that nearly decimated the Chinookan population by almost 90%.

In 1843, William Overton and Asa Lovejoy floated down the Willamette and came to this same spot. Overton laid claim to 640 acres of land that included the waterfront of the Willamette and the timbered hills beyond. He reportedly didn't have the necessary 25-cent filing fee for the claim, so in exchange for paying the fee, Lovejoy was given half of Overton's claim. They kept busy the next few years clearing trees, making roads, and building the first structures.

Two years later, Overton planned to move to California and sold his half of the land to Francis Pettygrove of Portland, Maine, for 50 dollars. In deciding a proper name for The Clearing, Lovejoy insisted that Boston, his hometown, was the best name, while Pettygrove urged that Portland was more appropriate. By the flip of a copper penny, Pettygrove won two out of three tosses and Portland, Oregon, was born.

BOSTON, OREGON?

Just think what Portland would be like today if Asa Lovejoy had won the coin toss and the city was named Boston, Oregon. It's interesting to surmise if the influence of a city's namesake can change the way a city may evolve. Would there be buildings built to resemble buildings from Boston, Massachusetts? Would any cultural attributes of one city be inherited by another?

A GROWING CITY

Within the next five years and fueled by the discovery of gold in California, the city grew quickly. Fishing, lumber, wheat, cattle, railroads, and the two rivers made Portland become the second largest city in the Northwest. The stumps of trees that had been cleared so quickly as the city expanded were painted white so they would be visible when navigating the muddy streets, giving the city one of its first nicknames—"Stumptown."

With the wave of prosperity and prospects came thousands of immigrants from around the world as well as Americans from the East. Boardinghouses surged with mostly male residents, and businesses boomed to support the new people. At the same time, the original landowners and wealthy began to move their mansions west toward the hills for more space.

SHANGHAI TUNNELS

In the early days of Portland, a network of underground tunnels were built as storage and a way to move goods from the wharf. But they were also used for kidnapping drunk or drugged men from establishments in Old Town. These men would be shuttled through tunnels beneath the saloons, boardinghouses, businesses, and hotels, and unwittingly placed on one of the many sailing ships desperate for crew. Brokers were paid handsomely for "shanghaiing" these crewmembers through what became known as the Shanghai Tunnels, which can still be toured.

A large influx of Chinese and Japanese immigrants arrived in the mid to late 1800s to help with the railroad boom and growing economies. By the 1920s, a bustling Chinatown and Japantown (Nihonmachi) grew to have their own schools, restaurants, and social organizations. But after the 1941 bombing of Pearl Harbor and Executive Order 9066 sent Japanese Americans to internment camps, Japantown in Portland disappeared. The remaining Chinatown neighborhood deteriorated as gambling, prostitution, and crime grew, and periodic flooding from the Willamette spurred the buildings' destruction.

The Chinatown Gate is at W Burnside and NW 4th Avenue.

The Lan Su Chinese Garden is at 239 NW Everett Street.

The mid-1900s was not kind to Old Town Chinatown, yet in time revitalization came. The term "Skid Row," as the neighborhood had come to be known, was upgraded to Old Town, and preservation of the cast-iron buildings led the area to be recognized as a historic district. The Chinatown Gate and Lan Su Chinese Garden are popular sites to visit, and the waterfront area, underneath the Burnside Bridge with the famous White Stag sign above, hosts one of the best arts and crafts markets in town, the Portland Saturday Market.

The Skidmore fountain is at SW 1st Avenue and Ankeny Street.

LLOYD DISTRICT

In the early 1900s, California rancher and oilman Ralph Lloyd moved across the Willamette from downtown Portland and today's Old Town Chinatown and bought parcels of land to build government buildings, shops, and apartments as a sort of "second downtown." But the city and residents were not as enchanted with his plan and his ideas never panned out. After he died, Lloyd's daughters finished one of their father's hotels and opened in 1960 the Lloyd Center, Oregon's largest mall today, complete with an ice rink. Today, Lloyd is also home to the Oregon Convention Center, The Rose Quarter (which includes the Moda Center, the Veterans Memorial Coliseum, the Theater of the Clouds, and the Exhibit Hall and the Rose Quarter Commons), and Portland Institute for Contemporary Art.

SCAVENGER HUNT

Head on a scavenger hunt at the Portland Saturday Market and sketch one-of-a-kind items made by Portland's very own crafters and makers.

Best-smelling item

Most glittery find

Spiciest food around

Something red

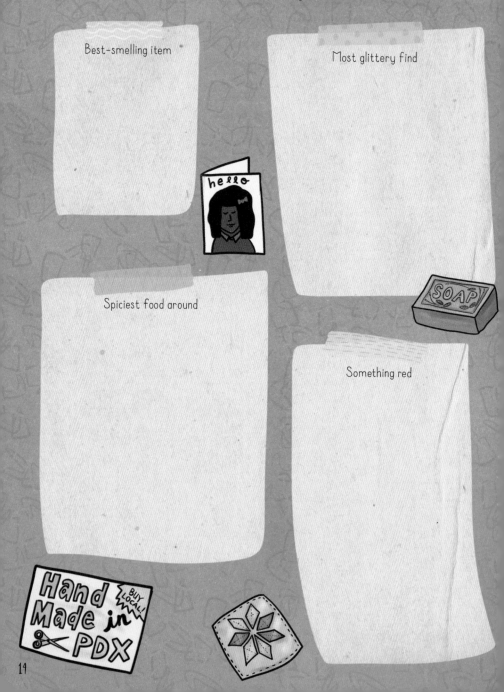

Oddest creation

Most popular

It's alive!

Handcrafted from wood

EVERY WEEKEND
MARCH - CHRISTMAS EVE

The Portland
Saturday Market
is at 2 SW Naito
Parkway.

15

SW: DOWNTOWN

Although downtown Portland is not nearly as residential as neighboring areas, wandering the streets and discovering some of the landmarks will show that community is clearly important to the city. This city's residents desired places where all could hang out, and they got them!

The Pioneer Courthouse is at 700 SW 6th Avenue.

PIONEER COURTHOUSE SQUARE

Pioneer Courthouse Square's site was initially Hotel Portland, built in 1882 by railroad tycoon Henry Villard. Villard went broke during construction, yet in community fashion the project was taken over by local investors and opened in 1890. It was a grand hotel for the day, with lavish ballrooms and a palm-lined courtyard entrance, and it even hosted 11 US presidents.

But over time the hotel began to physically deteriorate. By 1950, the hotel closed and was replaced a year later by a two-story parking garage for Portland's own Meier & Frank department store, called "One of America's Great Stores." (Meier & Frank's deep city roots go back to 1857 when Aaron Meier began selling goods on Front Street.) When the city talked about growing the parking garage to 11 stories, the community rallied and called instead for a central public space all could enjoy.

In 1984, the parking structure was replaced with Pioneer Courthouse Square, the new hub of downtown nicknamed "Portland's Living Room." There are events and food options offered year round at this site, including food trucks, farmers markets, rallies, concerts, and cultural festivals.

COMMUNITY PLACES

Portland's Living Room is not the only community-friendly place to visit in downtown. Here are a few sites to explore in this neighborhood that embraces this fellowship.

The Old Church is at 1422 SW 11th Avenue.

THE OLD CHURCH Built in 1882, this Carpenter Gothic–style building was first a Presbyterian church and is now a nonprofit that hosts concerts, storytelling events, lectures, and more. Listed on the National Register of Historic Places, it is fittingly named the Old Church as it is the oldest church building in downtown.

ART IN THE LIVING ROOM

In Portland's Living Room, J. Seward Johnson's "Allow Me" statue shows a man offering his umbrella, and Soderstrom's Architects' Bronze Chess Board inspires a friendly game. Tiles illustrate Portland's history, and a weather machine announces the day's forecast at noon. There are commemorative bricks that residents have purchased to stake their claim in the square as well as the Mile Post Sign, directing to places near and far, including the nine sister cities of Portland. Snap a selfie with the "Allow Me" man, take a photo of chess players, or record the noontime forecast to capture your time in Portland's Living Room.

17

SOUTH PARK BLOCKS In 1852 settler Daniel Lownsdale dedicated 11 blocks of his land to be a greenspace promenade running from what is now Portland State University to the center of town. The South Park Blocks, as they are known, are lined with prominent buildings and public art. At the south end is Oregon's largest museum, the Portland Art Museum, which recognizes the Indigenous Peoples of the region, and the city's largest farmers market, the Portland Farmers Market.

MILL ENDS PARK In 1946, *Oregon Journal* writer Dick Fagan noticed a hole in a median in the street outside his office. The proposed light post there was never built, so Fagan beautified the 452-square-inch (approximately 2 feet) spot with flowers and plants, and wrote a story of how leprechauns inhabited the area. Considered the world's smallest park, Mill Ends Park sometimes displays miniature additions from the community, like small statues, mini protests (including signs), and even a swimming pool at one time!

Mills End Park is at SW Naito Parkway and Taylor Street.

BENSON BUBBLERS The story goes that in the early 1900s, Simon Benson, a lumber baron, wanted to curb his mill workers' drinking. When he noticed it was hard to find fresh drinking water fountain, he donated $10,000 to the city to buy and install bronze drinking fountains. These ornate fountains (with more added over the years) can now be found throughout the neighborhood.

THE GREAT PLANK ROAD (CANYON ROAD)

When Daniel Lownsdale bought Francis Pettygrove's claim of The Clearing (the site that was later named Portland) along the Willamette River, he saw a huge opportunity for the area by connecting the agriculturally rich Tualatin Valley (over the west hills) to the docks along the Willamette. Not only did the growing Portland population need the fresh farm goods, but booming cities like San Francisco also needed produce and grains. Construction began on the Great Plank Road (now Canyon Road) using planks to help wagons navigate the often muddy and rugged terrain. Within only a decade much of the road deteriorated, but in recent years some of these planks have been rediscovered.

The Great Plank Road plaque is at 1219 SW Park Avenue.

TOM MCCALL WATERFRONT PARK

Portland took decades to reclaim its waterfront after the city cut off its own access to the Willamette. With a focus on inland developments, the city had built a seawall to prevent flooding in the 1920s and then built Harbor Drive in the 1940s. It wasn't until the 1970s with the addition of the Eastbank Freeway/I-5 did the city finally agree to remove Harbor Drive, and a public space beside the river developed. In 1984, Tom McCall Waterfront Park opened, named after Governor Tom McCall who backed the beautification plan. The park has many fountains and memorials along a long path that joggers, bikers, and walkers flock to on a sunny day.

PORTLANDIA

Crouching on top of the Portland Building with a trident in hand, the roughly 50-foot female statue (if she were standing) has become a symbol for the city. Artist Raymond Kaskey reportedly created this statute based on the figure of "Miss Commerce" in the city seal. It is the second-largest hammered copper statue in the US, the Statue of Liberty being the largest. Nearby is a plaque with a poem written by local lawyer and writer Ronald Talney, which was chosen out of over 900 other poems entered in a contest.

OVERHEARD IN THE SQUARE

Eavesdrop on conversations in the city's living room and fill out the speech bubbles below with interesting stories you may hear. Snippets of overheard dialog can give a little peek into the real lives of locals and perhaps even inspire a memorable or hilarious fictitious story!

WHAT'S THE STORY?

NW: PEARL DISTRICT

From train yards and warehouses to a vibrant gem of a neighborhood, the Pearl District is a story of how a once prosperous neighborhood can fall into disrepair and desertion, then be reenergized by Portland's creative residents to be reborn as a booming artsy enclave.

NORTH END

The Pearl initially emerged from a five-block public park in the North End known as the North Park Blocks. The park amid housing became the perfect impetus to creating a neighborhood for working class and middle-class families and immigrants to enjoy businesses such as a grocery store, a brewery, a saloon, and a laundry right next to homes.

Then the railroad boom came in the 1880s, taking over the shipping industry as the prime way to transport goods across the country. The railroad yard and accompanying buildings, warehouses, and switching yards soon took up a large portion of the area. Opened in 1896, Portland Union Station brought even more trains to the area, and many residents scattered to more family-friendly neighborhoods of Portland. Big businesses moved in to load and distribute goods easily, including furniture warehouses, plumbing suppliers, and a drug company. With all the industry, the area became known as the Northwest Industrial Triangle.

Portland Union Station is at 800 NW 6th Avenue.

FROM INDUSTRY TO ART

Things began to change from the 1950s to the 1970s. As railways fell out of use, industrial businesses moved their facilities to less populated suburbs, and the freeway (with its elevated sections and off- and on-ramps) tore up what little cohesiveness was left of the area.

But revitalization wasn't far behind. In the late 1970s and 1980s, some developers and investors who were inspired by New York's Soho's warehouse-to-loft conversions saw great opportunity in Portland's neglected warehouse neighborhood. Zoning laws were updated as warehouses became the perfect live/work situation. The arts community set up shop and galleries opened. The neighborhood was renamed "The Pearl," after gallery owner Thomas Augustine's inspirational and artistic friend, Pearl Marie Amhara, and the thought that when he looked at the old crusty buildings and the creative artists inside it was like a pearl hidden in an oyster. Once desolate, the industrious Pearl flourishes today with upscale shops, restaurants, galleries, and breweries for visitors to enjoy.

POWELL'S CITY OF BOOKS

Hailed as one of the best bookstores in America, Powell's City of Books is one of the top destinations in Portland and played a part in the rise of the Pearl. In 1971 Walter Powell bought a former car dealership in what was the Northwest Industrial District and opened a used bookstore there. A few years later, his son Michael joined him and continued to expand their book collection to become a "city of books." Covering a full city block, Powell's is a book lover's paradise, with color-coded rooms containing thousands of different sections of new and used books.

Powell's Books is at 1005 W Burnside Street.

BREW IT YOURSELF

The Pearl is also home to the Brewery Blocks (see page 98). In fact, there are over 70 microbreweries in the whole city of Portland! Join in on the beer-making adventure and create your own brew. Define your style of beer, choose the flavors, invent your brewery name, list your beer brands, and design a bottle label. Perhaps while at one of the brew pubs in the Pearl, shop your ideas around and see if any of them become a hit!

BREW STYLE

- [ ] PALE LAGER
- [ ] BLONDE ALE
- [ ] PALE ALE / IPA
- [ ] AMBER ALE
- [ ] RED ALE
- [ ] BROWN ALE
- [ ] PORTER
- [ ] STOUT
- [ ] OTHER:

SIGNATURE FLAVORS

Check all that apply.

- [ ] CRISP
- [ ] HOP
- [ ] MALT
- [ ] ROAST
- [ ] SOUR
- [ ] HERBAL
- [ ] CLEAN
- [ ] FRUITY
- [ ] SHARP

- [ ] HAZY
- [ ] SPICY
- [ ] BALANCED
- [ ] LIGHT BODIED
- [ ] TOASTED
- [ ] CREAMY
- [ ] CHOCOLATE
- [ ] STRONG
- [ ] PEPPERY

- [ ] BITTER
- [ ] CARMEL
- [ ] CIRTUSY
- [ ] FLORAL
- [ ] SOUR
- [ ] INTENSE
- [ ] SYRUPY
- [ ] OTHER:

BREWERY NAME

Brewery names vary wildly. They may include a name (your name, a historic person's name, a pet name), a location (country, state, city, street), and may also include an adjective(s) describing the overall styling of your beer or witty uniqueness. For example, your brewery could be named Polished Pearl's Brewing Company or Flanders Flying Squirrel Brew House. Write the name of your brewery below.

SIGNATURE BEER NAMES

List the name of your beer selection below.

DESIGN YOUR BOTTLE LABEL!

NW: ALPHABET DISTRICT, NOB HILL & SLABTOWN

Northwest Portland is a combination of several historic neighborhoods where the boundaries between each area are somewhat blurred. There is the famous Alphabet District, named for the streets that run north to south and follow an A-to-Z pattern (yet ironically don't include a Z). Within those streets is upscale Nob Hill, filled with historic homes and two trendy commercial streets, NW 21st Avenue and NW 23rd Avenue. And finally, at the north end of the area and the end of the alphabet is the once industrious neighborhood known as Slabtown.

ALPHABET DISTRICT ORIGINS

It was Captain John Couch who platted the Northwest Portland neighborhood and started the letter streets trend. In 1865 he started with A Street and finished with K Street. Within four years, he extended his subdivision with streets L to O. In 1891 (after Couch's passing), the city council decided to rename the streets in honor of Portland pioneers

THE SIMPSONS

Flanders, Kearney, Lovejoy, and Quimby Streets—notice a theme? References from *The Simpsons* and from its Portland creator Matt Groening's life are scattered throughout the city, including the name of the street he grew up on (Evergreen Terrace) and the names of his family members (Homer, Marge, Lisa, and Maggie). Groening's alma mater Lincoln High School (SW 18th Avenue near Salmon Street) even has a Bart Simpson drawing etched in the sidewalk.

and landowners. A Street became Ankeny for a riverboat captain, B Street became Burnside for a Portland Merchant, C Street became Couch for Captain Couch, and so on.

PRESTIGE ON NOB HILL

Although Couch's platted subdivision was part of the initial settlement of Portland, the bulk of the city's population remained closer to the river in Old Town and the Pearl. Then horse-drawn streetcars in the 1880s dramatically changed the Northwest District by making the "outskirts" of the growing city accessible. Homes for middle- and upper-class families filled the area, while the most wealthy and prosperous Portlanders (called the "Merchant Princes") moved westward and built even statelier homes with turrets, gables, and grand porches. Quickly the area took on the name "Nob Hill," after the wealthy neighborhood in San Francisco.

Chapman Elementary School is at 1445 NW 26th Avenue.

THE SWIFT SWARM

People flock in droves during the month of September to Northwest Portland to see a flock of a different kind, the Vaux Swift bird. Since the 1980s, a population of these birds has found the perfect place to roost for the night in an old chimney at the Chapman Elementary School. As sunset approaches, thousands of swifts flap overhead and start to swirl to enter the chimney. Watching this phenomenon will be quite memorable, so check Portland Audubon's website for more info.

SLABTOWN'S NAME

Slabtown, just north of Nob Hill, saw a different type of growth. In the latter half of the 1800s, sawmills were big business in Portland. Lumber was used to build homes and businesses, create railroad ties, "pave" sidewalks throughout the city, and was shipped to other locations outside of Portland. Working-class families came to work in these mills and in other manufacturing plants. Many of these hard workers were immigrants from Ireland, Slavic countries, Germany, and Sweden, and they built small homes with outhouses to live in near the mills. The neighborhood earned the name Slabtown after the leftover round bark cuttings called slabs that remained once the core lumber had been milled from a tree trunk. These slabs would be stacked in tall piles in front of homes to use for heat or to run machinery.

LEWIS & CLARK CENTENNIAL EXPOSITION

In 1905 Portland hosted its only world fair, the Lewis and Clark Centennial Exposition, to celebrate 100 years since the Lewis and Clark Expedition. Guild's Lake in Slabtown was the site chosen to build the exposition because it not only offered the open space at the time but also was accessible by trolley line and steamers on the Willamette.

With exhibitions from 16 states and 21 different countries, plus an amusement park, a blimp excursion, concerts, and more, the fair attracted nearly 1.6 million visitors. But today only a few buildings still exist from the fair, and unfortunately Guild's Lake has long been filled in and converted for industrial uses.

GELATINE

CHANGE IN THE NORTHWEST

Cinema 21 is at
616 NW 21st Avenue.

Meanwhile, Nob Hill began to grow as upper- and middle-class families came to live in the area. There was a construction surge of apartment buildings, residential hotels, and homes, with some of the stately mansions moved and others torn down to build multi-family buildings. A new type of affluent living was introduced, with elevators in some of the buildings. The very wealthy moved on while Nob Hill continued to become more densely populated and businesses grew, bringing parking lots with them. In the 1970s some of the remaining old historic homes were fixed up and older apartment buildings were revitalized to attract a new generation.

Today, the Alphabet District and Nob Hill are bustling neighborhoods. NW 23rd Avenue, sometimes called the "trendy third," is lined with upscale boutique stores and retail shops, cafés, and restaurants. NW 21st Avenue caters more toward entertainment with bars, pubs, nightclubs, and a movie theater. Wandering off the main streets is also a treat where you can still spot some of the beautiful historic homes that defined this neighborhood.

Nob Hill Bar & Grill is at
937 NW 23rd Avenue.

DESIGN THE ABCS

Make an alphabet that is uniquely Portland! As you wander through Northwest Portland, make a sketch of each letter you see. The letter may be on a neon sign, in an old apartment building name, in a crack in the sidewalk, or made from the shape of a building. Keep your eyes peeled. You'll be surprised how many letters appear once you start the hunt!

30

SW: GOOSE HOLLOW, SOUTHWEST HILLS, HOMESTEAD & SOUTH WATERFRONT

Bordering bustling downtown Portland to the south and west are Goose Hollow, Southwest Hills, Homestead, and South Waterfront. The stories from each neighborhood not only show the love Portlanders have for their beautiful hills, views, and waterfront but also reveal their progressive spirit and dedication to environmental and sustainable practices.

GOOSE HOLLOW

Just as Old Town, downtown, and the Northwest neighborhoods in Portland were being settled, so too was the Southwest. Early white settlers built cabins and barns, and German, Swiss, and Italian immigrants opened dairy and vegetable farms. In 1845 in an area hollowed out by Tanner Creek, west of downtown, Daniel Lownsdale established one of the only tanneries west of the Rocky Mountains. Farms (many rented by Chinese farmers) covered the hills, and blue-collar laborers took

up residence in the lower areas near the creek. By 1875, this area was named Goose Hollow after different flocks of geese began to mix and their owners started a ruckus about who owned which geese!

SOUTHWEST HILLS

South of Goose Hollow are the Southwest Hills, a lush area home to some of the wealthiest in Portland. On a clear day one can see Mount Hood, Mount St. Helens, and other peaks. In the early 1900s, the Portland Railway Light & Power Company built an amusement park

there to attract riders to their newly opened streetcar line. Council Crest Amusement Park was touted as the "Dreamland of the Northwest," where hundreds of Portlanders could play at "the top of the city." Its main attractions included a boat ride called "Trip Up the Columbia" and the L. A. Thompson Scenic Railway. The fun ended in 1929 when the park closed, but the views atop Council Crest Park are still worth the visit.

HOMESTEAD

Neighboring the Southwest Hills, Homestead was originally a 298-acre land claim purchased in 1857 by Phillip Marquam, who platted a subdivision referred to as "Portland City Homestead." Despite some undevelopable land, the area has grown into a diverse neighborhood with residential living and beautiful forests and parks (including Marquam Nature Park), as well as with large institutions, namely Oregon Health and Science University (OHSU) and the Veterans Medical Center. OHSU is located on top of Marquam Hill, which is now affectionately known as "Pill Hill."

This hilltop complex also offers easy access to the South Waterfront land along the Willamette River by being a terminus to Portland's novel Aerial Tram. Opened in 2006, the tram has been praised for its unique addition to the Portland landscape as well as the revitalization of the fledgling South Waterfront neighborhood.

The Portland Aerial Tram is at 3303 S Bond Avenue.

SOUTH WATERFRONT

South Waterfront is one of the largest urban renewal redevelopment projects in Portland's history. The first businesses here include the Portland Lumber Company, which provided heat and electricity to the city's growing downtown. Having access to the Willamette River encouraged other industrial businesses in the shipping trade, such as metal fabrication, chemical plants, and salvaging companies, to inhabit this area through the turn of the century and into the early 1900s. During and after World War II, the location was used for ship and barge building. Then with the arrival of two freeways, Harbor Drive and I-5, the area became completely cut off and the brownfield was left unused.

As urban renewal projects soared across the country in the late 1970s into the 2000s, developers saw potential in renewing the South Waterfront District into a vibrant area filled with mixed-use housing and commercial and retail areas. They restored the waterfront with friendly transit options, all while committing to environmentally friendly and sustainable development practices. The project provided jobs, housing, and acres of safe, rejuvenated public open spaces. Today the gleaming glass towers of the South Waterfront neighborhood have proved the redevelopment to be a success.

TILIKUM CROSSING

Named from the Chinook word for "people," Tilikum Crossing is one of the only major US bridges designated solely for public transportation, pedestrians, and bikes, and does not allow cars. The bridge connects the South Waterfront with the Central Eastside across the Willamette, providing an environmentally friendly addition to the city without the noise and pollution that cars bring. Also, the bridge encourages better land usage and waterfront development as it does not need extensive on- and off-ramps for car access.

THE BRIDGES OF PORTLAND

With 15 bridges total, Portland rightfully earned the nicknames Bridge City and Bridgetown! See how many bridges you see or cross as you travel around the city.

ACROSS THE WILLAMETTE RIVER IN PORTLAND

- St. Johns Bridge (1931)
- Burlington Northern Railroad Bridge 5.1 (1908)
- Fremont Bridge (1973)
- Broadway Bridge (1913)
- Steel Bridge (1912)
- Burnside Bridge (1926)
- Morrison Bridge (1958)
- Hawthorne Bridge (1910)
- Marquam Bridge (1966)
- Tilikum Crossing: Bridge of the People (2015)
- Ross Island Bridge (1922)
- Sellwood Bridge (1925/2016)

ACROSS THE COLUMBIA RIVER IN PORTLAND TO WASHINGTON

- Burlington Northern Railroad Bridge 9.6, also known as Columbia River Railroad Bridge (1908)
- Interstate Bridge (1917)
- Glenn Jackson Bridge (1982)

FOUND OBJECT

milk
bread
tomatoes
apples

old list

In the Portland spirit of environmental awareness and sustainable living,

Rainbow Collage

Look for pieces of nature in all different colors—leaves, berries, nuts, acorns, flower petals, and more. Once found, arrange in rainbow order and snap a picture.

pine needles

stones

twig

trash

fern

NATURE ART

gravel

here are some creative projects to do with objects found on this trip.

berries

Rock Art

Arrange found small stones in a stack or pattern for others to enjoy as they pass by.

Nature Art

Gather various elements in nature, and arrange as a picture. Take a photo to remember your artwork.

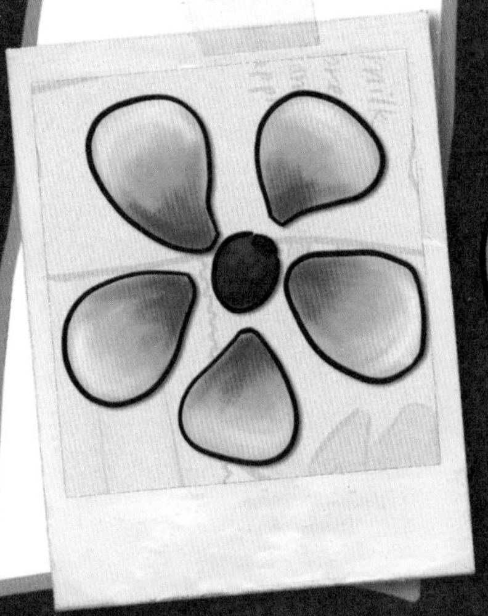

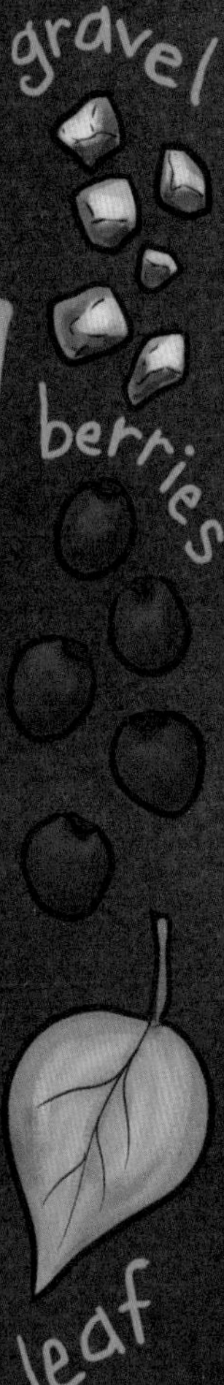

leaf

petals

gum wrapper

found objects

SE: SELLWOOD-MORELAND

With its small-town feel, the Sellwood-Moreland neighborhood in Portland is a welcoming home for families and young professionals. It has an easygoing vibe, with walkable streets filled with restaurants, bars, coffee shops, parks, a wildlife refuge, an amusement park, and too many antique shops to count. Given the urban and suburban mix, it is not surprising to learn it was first settled as an independent city.

AN EARLY SETTLEMENT ALONG THE WILLAMETTE

In the mid-1840s migrants came on the Oregon Trail from the East and settled along the shores of the Willamette River. The area was prime for logging, farming, and trade with the closest city just south of the area, Milwaukie. The Willamette and Milwaukie Road (which still exists today and is a main artery in the neighborhood) provided easy access between the growing communities, bringing prosperity in those early years.

Sellwood didn't get its name until Reverend John Sellwood sold his 321-acre claim to Sellwood Real Estate Company in 1882. The real estate company provided free ferry rides from downtown to get across the Willamette River in order to attract new buyers. Then in 1892 Sellwood became even more connected to downtown when one of the first interurban rail lines in the Pacific Northwest, The Portland Sellwood and Milwaukie Railway, brought streetcars to the area. The popular rail line also gave people access to the City View Race Track, a horse racetrack near today's Sellwood Riverfront Park. Though in the 1880s Portland officials tried to rid their city of gambling, drinking establishments, and

uncivilized behavior, the east bank of the Willamette was seemingly far enough away from Portland where the debauchery could continue!

THE GROWTH OF SELLWOOD AND SURROUNDING NEIGHBORHOODS

As Sellwood continued to grow and serve families of mill workers and crews who operated and maintained expanding streetcar lines, so did the neighboring area of Moreland (which includes Eastmoreland and Westmoreland). By the turn of the twentieth century, this farming area was platted into subdivisions where developers promised modern amenities like sidewalks and curbs. Eastmoreland, with its proximity to the newly founded Reed Institute (Reed College), was compared to other neighborhoods in close proximity to small universities, such as California's Palo Alto and Stanford University. With a golf course also in the area, Eastmoreland and Westmoreland attracted white-collared professionals who could take the streetcars to work in Portland.

The opening of the Sellwood Bridge in 1925 continued to bring people to Sellwood-Moreland. But once the Great Depression arrived, followed by World War II, growth of the area began to wane. Businesses closed, people moved away, and storefronts emptied. Fortunately, toward the end of the century, things began to turn around as antique shops opened in affordable spaces, historic homes began to be renovated, and new stores and restaurants arrived.

WILLAMETTE RIVER
SELLWOOD
BRIDGE
BUILT AND MAINTAINED
BY MULTNOMAH COUNTY

REED COLLEGE

SELLWOOD-MORELAND TODAY

One could spend a whole day browsing the fantastic antique shops in Sellwood-Moreland, or visiting historic sites like the historic Oaks Pioneer Church and the single-screen cinema, Moreland Theater. Many also like to explore nature at the Oaks Bottom Wildlife Refuge, which offers several trails to wander through woods, meadows, and marshlands to observe a wide variety of species. This relaxed and easygoing neighborhood where old-time amusement prevails is the perfect place to explore to get a taste of Portland's family-friendly vibe.

Moreland Theater is at 6712 SE Milwaukie Avenue.

Oaks Bottom Wildlife Refuge is at Sellwood Boulevard and SE 7th Avenue.

OAKS PARK

Where the fun never ends!

Oaks Park is at 7805 SE Oaks Park Way.

THE OAKS

Oaks Amusement Park opened on May 30, 1905, on the shores of the Willamette River in the Sellwood neighborhood. It is one of the 10 oldest amusement parks in the country and is still open today!

Fred Morris, president of the Oregon Water Power and Railway Company, invested in developing an amusement park to boast streetcar ridership. He also wanted to take advantage of tourists who were about to arrive for the Lewis and Clark Centennial Exposition being built at the same time in Northwest Portland. The Oaks opened two days ahead of the exposition and was a hit with over 300,000 visitors in the first season. The park also took advantage of the exposition's closure afterward and purchased some of their amenities, including the Whirlwind ride, lamp posts, benches, and a gazebo.

Despite floods and fires, economic depressions, and more, Oaks Park still thrives, continuing to entertain Portlanders and visitors alike for over a century. Be sure to visit its roller rink, the largest in the Northwest and oldest west of the Mississippi!

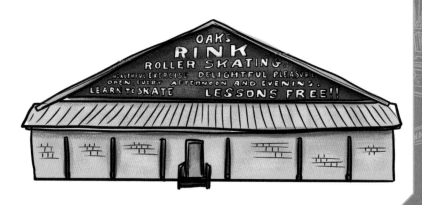

OAKS RINK
ROLLER SKATING.
HEALTHFUL EXERCISE — DELIGHTFUL PLEASURE
OPEN EVERY AFTERNOON AND EVENING.
LEARN TO SKATE   LESSONS FREE!!

PARK MAP

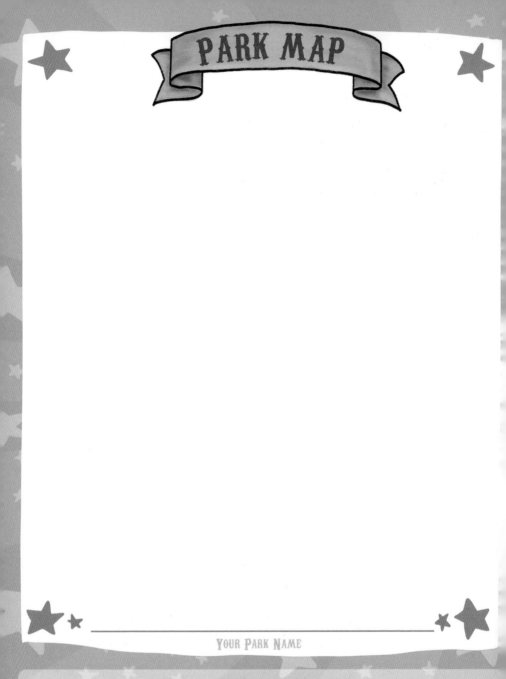

FUN & GAMES AT THE PARK

In the spirit of long-lasting Oaks Park, create your own Portland-themed amusement park. Draw a map of the park and include details of the rides, entertainment, and games that remind you of your time discovering the different areas of Portland. Don't forget to come up with some signature foods served at your park—perhaps puffy blue cotton candy clouds (for Portland's notorious rainy weather) or home-brewed root beer in the spirit of Portland's breweries!

SE: HAWTHORNE DISTRICT

Hawthorne isn't officially a "neighborhood" of Portland but a district, with Hawthorne Boulevard being the main artery running through the Southeast neighborhoods of Buckman, Ladd's Addition, Hosford-Abernathy, Sunnyside, Richmond, and Mount Tabor from approximately 11th to 55th Avenues. Many Portlanders love to spend time here because the street overflows with artsy coolness, from hip restaurants and funky shops to loads of thrift stores.

HAWTHORNE'S BEGINNINGS

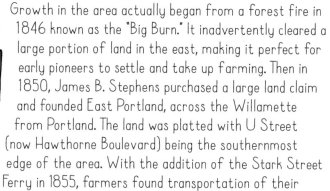

Growth in the area actually began from a forest fire in 1846 known as the "Big Burn." It inadvertently cleared a large portion of land in the east, making it perfect for early pioneers to settle and take up farming. Then in 1850, James B. Stephens purchased a large land claim and founded East Portland, across the Willamette from Portland. The land was platted with U Street (now Hawthorne Boulevard) being the southernmost edge of the area. With the addition of the Stark Street Ferry in 1855, farmers found transportation of their goods across the river to Portland easier than before.

By the late 1850s, Dr. J. C. Hawthorne cofounded Oregon's first mental hospital in what is now the Hawthorne District. With the hospital's opening, U Street was renamed to Asylum Avenue. Almost all the diagnoses of the time are classified differently today, but the hospital was considered progressive then and one of a kind for the era. After the hospital moved to Salem, the street's name was then changed to Hawthorne Boulevard in honor of the famed doctor.

LONE FIR PIONEER CEMETERY

The historic Lone Fir Pioneer Cemetery in Central Eastside is home to more than 30,000 souls. Named after a single fir tree on the site, which amazingly still exists today, the cemetery's first burial was Emmor Stephens, James Stephens's father, in 1846. The nearby hospital set up by Dr. J. C. Hawthorne also buried 132 patients there, including Hawthorne himself. Along with pioneers and prominent community figures such as Portland cofounder Asa Lovejoy, James Stephens, mayors, governors, and firefighters, the cemetery is also the resting place of everyday Portland citizens throughout history, like hardworking Chinese immigrants, artists, poets, brewers, and more.

Lone Fir Cemetery is at 649 SE 26th Avenue.

As you wander through the cemetery, take note of the names on the gravestones and mausoleums. Use your imagination and combine different first and last names to create colorful characters. With the new names, jot down a few words or craft an imaginary short story about their life in Portland in whatever era you choose.

TRANSPORTATION TRANSFORMATION

As seen in other neighborhoods in Portland, it was the advent of the streetcar during the 1880s, as well as the opening of the first version of Morrison Bridge in 1887, that really transformed the area. Over the next several decades the farming community in the Hawthorne District transformed into suburban living. Subdivisions of housing drew people east, followed by small businesses along Hawthorne Boulevard to serve the new inhabitants. With the relatively expansive amount of land in this eastern portion of this city, the population soared.

Hawthorne District underwent another transformation with the arrival of automobiles. As the streetcar lines aged and tracks got more expensive to maintain, buses and automobiles began to fill the thoroughfare, making it one of the busiest in the city. The street was widened, gas stations and automobile-friendly areas proliferated, sidewalks were reduced in size to make way for parking, and parking lots were added. The district evolved during tumultuous times of economic booms, busts, and wars. The postwar working-class area saw an influx of hippies during the 1970s that began to define the bohemian spirit that lives on today. Yet despite all the changes, one can still see historic buildings along Hawthorne that hark back to its roots.

Today, the scene on Hawthorne Boulevard echoes the "weirdness" that Portland is so often labeled. The eccentric area welcomes all, from hippies to hipsters, to anyone else who may want to visit. There's something there for everyone: plant-based eateries, live music, funky boutiques, an acrobat theater, a perfume shop, a cupcake shop, a cider house, an outer space–themed lounge, the historic Bagdad Theater, and apparently more vintage shops than any other place in the city. What's not to love?!

Bagdad Theater & Pub is at 3702 SE Hawthorne Boulevard.

RECYCLE, REUSE, RECREATE

Get into the green Portland mindset! Find an item at a vintage store and brainstorm different uses for it beyond the item's actual purpose. If you broke it or deconstructed it, what would you get? If you added things to it, would it be something else? Use the list below to fill in your ideas.

1.

2.

3.

4.

5.

6.

7.

8.

9.

10.

Bonus ideas:

LADD'S ADDITION

If you notice some odd diagonal streets that don't follow the typical grid layout in the Hosford-Abernethy neighborhood bordering SE Hawthorne Boulevard, you have found Ladd's Addition. Named after landowner and prominent Portlander William S. Ladd, this historic district is Portland's oldest planned neighborhood—and one of the oldest in the western United States.

The diagonal layout with a traffic circle in the middle is said to be inspired by Washington, DC, albeit on a much smaller scale. Many of the streets are named after trees, but Ladd did include some self-recognition with Ladd Avenue and Elliott Avenue (his wife's maiden name). Both the triangular rose gardens and prominent central garden, Ladd's Circle, are filled with roses, an aspect of the plan from the beginning.

Ladd Circle Park is at SE 16th Avenue and Harrison Street.

TREASURE HUNT AT THE THRIFT STORE

The thrill in thrift store shopping is finding that one-of-a-kind item. You never know what you'll find! While wandering on SE Hawthorne Boulevard, sketch a variety of interesting vintage items that catch your eye. Add a few notes alongside and give a story to your found object. Was it their favorite item? Writing the stories may be just as fun as sketching the item!

Who previously owned this?

Who does this item remind you of?

Where has this lived before?

Where was this originally bought?

What events has this been to?

What is the story behind this item?

SE: DIVISION/CLINTON

In the inner southeast neighborhoods of Richmond and Hosford-Abernethy lies the trendy Division/Clinton District. This commercial area retains an element of old charm yet bubbles with the city's characteristic hipness. Historic homes mix with swanky condos, and a plethora of shops, bars, and cafés satisfies the blend of inhabitants, from youthful singles to middle-aged empty nesters.

The district also declares its uniqueness with independent galleries, boutiques, fresh markets, food co-ops, a barbershop, and one of the oldest operating movie houses in the nation, Clinton Street Theater. Even though it's not recognized as a neighborhood of its own, it still draws the community for the annual Division/Clinton Street Fair and Parade in the summertime with performers, vendors, music, and, of course, food.

The Clinton Street Theater is at 2522 SE Clinton Street.

What really makes Division/Clinton stand out, though, is its incredible food scene. From Restaurant Row to Portland's Kitchen, Eat Street to the hottest food corridor in town, Division/Clinton offers a wide range of culinary treats and eating experiences whether you're looking for food carts or fine dining. So, how did Portland's food scene become so renowned?

THE PERFECT LOCATION

Surrounded by incredibly fertile land, including nearby Willamette Valley, crop lands and orchards make the farm-to-table culinary trend a given here, considering the farms are practically next to the tables! The city is also bordered by rivers and boasts an ocean of seafood nearby, plus the close forests are a forager's dream, filled with mushrooms, truffles, wild berries, roots, and nuts. With its sustainable and enterprising spirit, no wonder Portlanders are known to have their own vegetable gardens, backyard hives, chicken coops, and farm animals like rabbits and pygmy goats. Even City Hall has a veggie garden called the Better Together Garden, bursting with organic goodness in the center of downtown.

The Better Together Garden is at 1221 SW 4th Avenue.

LAND OF FOOD CARTS

Portland's unique food scene breaks all conventions. Sometimes food cart owners leap into the restaurant business—but restaurants turn to the food cart business too! Compared to the risky business endeavor of opening a restaurant, a food cart is much more accessible and inclusive for different income levels. City officials see the food cart culture as a positive aspect of Portland that can even rejuvenate seedy or abandoned areas, so they encourage food cart businesses by making it affordable to obtain the necessary permits.

In 2001, there were approximately 175 food carts in Portland. Jump forward to 2020 and you'll find around 600 food carts in the city with upwards of 500 operating at once. One could spend hours eating at these many food trucks or pods (a group of food carts or trucks). A day's menu may include a breakfast taco, comforting grilled cheese for lunch, and a spicy noodle bowl for dinner. Don't forget snacks, like shaved ice, gelato, churros, and a slice of homemade pie, to name a few! Portland's food carts don't seem to be plagued by all the same food options either and enjoy a healthy competition of sorts to come up with original dishes to serve.

Cartopia is at 1207 SE Hawthorne Boulevard.

A look at the food scene shows how the city embraces global cuisine and flavors as well as local delights, as anyone can see from the popularity of the fan-favorite Vietnamese fish sauce wings and the bacon maple bar doughnuts.
Yet this gastronomical town lacks pretension.
Despite the food tours (like Forktown), podcasts (Right at the Fork), blogs (Food Carts Portland), and a renowned food festival (Feast Portland Food and Drink Festival) dedicated to the city, Portlanders leave the restaurant snobs and highfalutin cuisine creations for other places and embrace delicious local food at the neighborhood level.

FOODIE'S DELIGHT

Here's just a little taste of the types of foods available in the district:

- vegan ice cream
- doughnuts
- moules (mussels)
- handmade corn tortillas
- bánh mi
- Israeli-inspired hummuses
- freshly baked bread
- Indian street food (chaat)
- Belgian waffles

- Scandinavian specialties
- egg scrambles
- fresh pies
- gourmet burgers
- Korean BBQ
- Vietnamese fish sauce wings (a legend in Portland!)

And don't forget drinks! There are plenty of unique beverages to sip:

- steeped tea
- fresh cider
- Portland brewed beer
- specialty coffee
- famous Oregon pinot

JAMES BEARD, "THE DEAN OF AMERICAN CUISINE"

With Portland's love of food, of course it's also the birthplace of the great renowned chef, teacher, and author James Beard. Born in Portland in 1903, Beard grew up being exposed to the area's food abundance. It's even reported he was able to recall his food memories at the Lewis and Clark Centennial Exposition in 1905 when he was only two years old! Although Beard left Portland relatively early in his career, his legacy of embracing and teaching the benefits of fresh, wholesome foods are akin to many principles of the Portland scene today.

DOUGHNUT DESIGN SPACE

These doughnut shops aren't anything like the ones from the old days. Pretty much anything goes on doughnuts in this town! Join the revolution and add your own doughnuts below with whatever fancies your taste buds. Remember, all bets are off when it comes to flavors!

SERVE IT UP!

Join the food truck revolution and create your own unique menu of what you would serve. Once your menu is decided, decorate your food truck.

Your Food Truck Name

Type of Food

- [ ] American
- [ ] Southern
- [ ] Southwestern
- [ ] Seafood
- [ ] Cakes, Pies, Cookies
- [ ] Ice Cream
- [ ] Mexican
- [ ] Mediterranean
- [ ] Greek
- [ ] Asian
- [ ] Sushi
- [ ] Indian
- [ ] Middle Eastern
- [ ] Other:

Style of Food

- [ ] Homestyle
- [ ] Farm Fresh
- [ ] Deep Fried
- [ ] BBQ
- [ ] Baked Goodness
- [ ] Ethnic
- [ ] Junk Food
- [ ] Grilled
- [ ] Healthy
- [ ] Vegan
- [ ] Vegetarian
- [ ] Meatatarian
- [ ] Sweet
- [ ] Other:

•MENU•

SE: CENTRAL EASTSIDE

The Central Eastside (also called Central Eastside Industrial District, or CEID) is a highly connected neighborhood with five bridges, loads of railroad tracks, a streetcar route, and plenty of warehouses. Revitalized industrial buildings provide the perfect live/work arrangement for artists and craftspeople, while renovated warehouses house high-tech startups and small businesses. Restaurants, clubs, and bars flourish, and the Oregon Museum of Science and Industry and the Oregon Rail Heritage Center draw crowds. CEID keeps true to its value of inclusiveness by supporting artists, businesses, and industry at all levels while reenergizing an age-old neighborhood.

The Oregon Rail Heritage Center is at 2250 SE Water Avenue.

PORTLAND CONNECTS & EXPANDS EAST

The riverfront across the Willamette from the newly developed town of Portland was a challenge to develop as it was mainly sloughs, marshes, and creeks. Despite this land issue, pioneer James B. Stephens knew being close to the river would be a boon. He platted some of his land there into blocks and launched Stephens Ferry (later renamed Stark Street Ferry) in 1848 to connect both sides of the river. In approximately 20 years, railroad tracks of the Oregon Central Railroad further linked this new town of East Portland with Portland and surrounding towns, including Salem. The plethora of fresh produce being moved along the river and railroad gave the Central Eastside the nickname of Produce Row.

URBAN RENEWAL

Until the 1980s, the Central Eastside looked pretty worn from decades of industrial business, freeways, railroads, and urbanization. But revitalization came, one highlight being the popular Oregon Museum of Science and Industry (OMSI). In 1992 OMSI busted out of its small location in Washington Park and opened in the CEID, taking over an old General Electric power plant and constructing new buildings to house several halls of interactive science exhibits and demonstrations, a large theater, a planetarium, and much more.

Another success in the CEID is the Vera Katz Eastbank Esplanade. Named after a former mayor, the bike and walking path along the river sports an incredible view of downtown and many of its bridges. It also includes a large floating walkway, reported to be the longest in the country, between Burnside and Steel Bridge that rises and falls with the tide to prevent flooding.

The Vera Katz Eastbank Esplanade is at SE Water Avenue and Hawthorne Boulevard.

There are old warehouses and buildings in the area refurbished in more recent years. Washington High School sat empty for decades before turning into Revolution Hall, a bustling venue for live entertainment. An old industrial laundry warehouse was converted into Yale Union, a center for contemporary art that supports emerging and unacknowledged artists. There are also longstanding businesses in the area that weathered through urbanization and stand today alongside their shiny new neighbors.

The Central Eastside continues to evolve and grow, yet remains primarily an industrial area providing Portlanders with job opportunities as well as tourist attractions, like the Stark's Vacuum Museum. Between the renovated warehouses and new developments, you're guaranteed to find office workers, craftspeople, and artists walking around. This blending of old and new, traditional and alternative, keeps the Central Eastside Industrial District grounded, yet uniquely cool.

CREATE A ZINE

In the heart of the CEID lives the Independent Publishing Resource Center (IPRC), a nonprofit committed to providing affordable workspace, tools, and resources to create independently published media and artwork, such as zines. At the IPRC there is a zine library with over 9,000 self-published creations!

Create a zine of your Portland experiences. You could highlight the artistic expression you saw throughout the city, or focus on the food you ate. You could draw miniature portraits of people you met, or comment on your feelings as you discover Portland. Use this space to jot down and sketch your ideas, then follow the instructions on the next page to make your own zine using a blank piece of paper.

My Zine Ideas

art • tools • tunes • murals • words

Perfectly PDX

things I saw

POEMS

POLITICS

randomness

FUEL & FOODS

SUBCULTURE

How to Make a Zine

1. Use an 8.5"x11" or 11"x17" sheet of paper.

2. Fold lengthwise.

3. Fold in half.

4. Fold in half again.

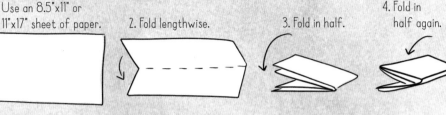

5. Open up and make a cut in the center along the center fold.

6. Fold lengthwise again and "pop open" along the cut center.

7. Refold to make a booklet.

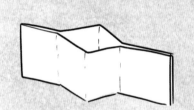

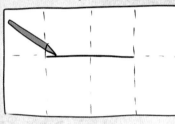

Recycled Paper Zine

Gather found papers while touring the city, preferably with little writing. Perhaps they're scraps from a paper bag, partially written lists, graph paper, or torn pieces from a hotel notepad. Put all the papers together and staple into a book. Trim with scissors to make even.

WHAT'S A ZINE?

A zine is a self-published, small-circulation work of text and images, somewhat like a mini magazine. A zine comes in many shapes and sizes, and can focus on arts, politics, music, and other subculture topics with drawings, poems, creative writing, and more. They're often reproduced by low-end means such as a photocopier and distributed in indie shops or via the web.

NE: ALBERTA ARTS DISTRICT

The Alberta Arts District is an eclectic area that connects the neighborhoods of Concordia, King, and Vernon in Northeast Portland. NE Alberta Street is the main drag, with roughly 20 blocks filled with a mix of ethnically diverse independent shops, restaurants, bars, and more. Given the artsy nature and emphasis on handcrafted uniqueness of the area, it's no surprise big-box stores are nowhere to be found; instead, colorful murals and newly renovated buildings stand alongside longstanding stores and local businesses.

BEFORE THE ARTS

Since the 1880s, Alberta had a diverse population, supporting immigrants from varied backgrounds with homes, stores, and varied places to worship. With the streetcar's arrival in 1903, more homes and storefronts were built, but it wasn't until the 1950s and 1960s that things began to decline.

A new freeway and large-scale commercial developments just south of Alberta Street were built and changed traffic patterns, diverting away the once steady stream of cars and in turn bringing less business to the street. These new developments also tore down many homes, displacing underrepresented groups and low-income families into the Alberta Street area. The displacement increased racial tensions and brought crime, violence, and vandalism to the neighborhood that escalated well into the 1980s.

THE COMMUNITY STEPS IN

When the community saw what their deteriorated neighborhood had become, it organized task forces to work with the city to help revitalize the area. In particular, artist and activist Roslyn Hill spearheaded long-lasting change. To maintain Black ownership of businesses on Alberta Street, she purchased a dilapidated building and converted it into a garden café for her neighbors. She continued to buy almost a dozen other buildings, fixing them up and renting them to fellow neighbors.

Bistros, taquerias, artist workspaces, coffee shops, and galleries started to open. By the late 1990s, businesses doubled on the street. Planning committees discussed the desire for murals and beautifying public areas, which, along with reasonable rents, soon brought artists in to set up shop. By 1997 Alberta had its very own art walk. Known as Last Thursday, the art walk started with only a small number of participants displaying and selling their art, but today the popular gathering hosts many artists, vendors, entertainment, and music.

Stay at the Caravan Tiny House Hotel, which is made up of trendy tiny houses, or see a show at the 1927 Alberta Rose Theatre, which hosts cabarets, concerts, and circus performances. Visit the nonprofit cycling shop Community Cycling Center, whose hope is for every Portlander to be able to own a bike, regardless of income or background. Eat at the Bollywood Theater, a restaurant that serves Indian street food and plays Bollywood films. Once overrun

The Alberta Rose Theatre is at 3000 NE Alberta Street.

with crime, the Alberta Arts District now showcases Portland's ambitious community coming together to create a funky, distinctive neighborhood.

The Community Cycling Center is at 1700 NE Alberta Street.

WHAT MAKES AN ARTS DISTRICT?

Alberta Street has many galleries, yet are there enough to make up an arts district? Portlanders argue an artsy neighborhood isn't defined by the number of galleries or museums along the street—it's about how the arts permeate the neighborhood. Along with Alberta's galleries, artist residences, and workspaces, the restaurants, stores, and bars also feature artworks on their walls. In a sense, the whole street is a gallery of sorts.

OPEN A GALLERY

You have just refurbished an old building on Alberta Street and are ready to open a new gallery. Decorate the walls of your space, keeping in mind the artsy soul of the district. Be creative and include all types of art forms (drawing, painting, collaging, etc.) and styles to create your personal gallery.

NE: GRANT PARK & HOLLYWOOD

From Grant Park's tree-lined streets and beautiful historic homes in Craftsman, Cape Cod, Bungalow, and Colonial styles, to Hollywood's Sandy Boulevard, a popular street bubbling with markets, shops, bars, and the outstanding and historic Hollywood Theatre, these neighborhoods are just the right spot if you're looking for a little nostalgia and charm.

GRANT PARK

Like most neighborhoods in Northeast Portland, Grant Park, named after Ulysses S. Grant, was once farmland. When the Broadway Line streetcar came, connecting the area to downtown, the neighborhood blossomed. Homes, businesses, schools, and a community park (also called Grant Park) ensured the area would be the family-friendly neighborhood it is still today.

HOLLYWOOD

Hollywood has a similar historic past. Originally it was part of the Rose City Park subdivision. In 1906, the Rose City Line streetcar came to Sandy Boulevard, and so too did families looking for a more suburban life. A cornerstone landmark to Sandy Boulevard was the Steigerwald Dairy Company opening in 1926, with its monolithic milk bottle on the corner of the building. (The milk bottle has evolved over the years, from milk to soda to beer, and now finally to a mortgage company sign.) Just down the street from the dairy company, the Hollywood Theatre

The Hollywood Theatre is at 4122 NE Sandy Boulevard.

opened in the same year with the showing of the silent movie *More Pay - Less Work*. This historic building is what the district is named after and still exists on Sandy Boulevard as a nonprofit that shows classic and contemporary films.

BEVERLY CLEARY

Beyond the charming streets and historic businesses, Grant Park and Hollywood are most famously known as the backdrop for children's author Beverly Cleary's series of books that feature fictional characters Henry Higgins and sisters Ramona and Beatrice "Beezus" Quimby who live on Klickitat Street. Cleary grew up in Grant Park with real-life Klickitat Street just a few blocks north. A number of the incidents in her books are inspired from her adventures in the neighborhood.

Both Hollywood and Grant Park neighborhoods pay tribute to their beloved author. The park Grant Park is not only filled with trees, a dog park, tennis courts, playgrounds, a pool, and an adjoining local high school, but is also home to the Beverly Cleary Sculpture Garden. The garden has three bronze statues: one of Henry, one of Ramona, and one of Ribsy, Henry's dog. There are fountains where kids can splash and play when the weather is warm, and tiles surrounding the area that are engraved with Cleary's book titles. In nearby Hollywood, the local public library branch has a map etched in a wall marking Beverly Cleary landmarks in the neighborhood. As progressive and hip as Portland may be, these tributes to Beverly Cleary and the nostalgic charm of these neighborhoods are a testament of the community also embracing simpler times.

The Beverly Cleary Sculpture Garden is near NE 33rd Avenue and Brazee Street.

NE Klickitat St 3300

WRITE LIKE BEVERLY CLEARY

Inspired by Beverly Cleary and her famous children's books, write a book summary for your own children's tale based on your time exploring Portland. Fill out the spaces below to brainstorm your story's setting, characters, and plot. Once complete, sketch the front cover on the next page.

Setting Details

Character Ideas

Story Arc: Plot, Conflict, Resolution

NORTH PORTLAND

North Portland (NoPo) is located at the confluence of the Willamette and Columbia Rivers. In NoPo one can find lakes, wetlands, marshes, sloughs, and even a neighborhood on an island. But what makes the area stand out as one of the most eclectic and coolest areas of Portland is the 11 individual neighborhoods and their communities.

JAMES JOHN

Thought to be the place where the Lewis and Clark Expedition camped when they explored the area in 1805, North Portland developed thanks to James John, who built a homestead here while pioneers such as Francis Pettygrove and John Couch were growing central Portland. Within five years, a dozen more families joined John and an eight-block townsite called St. Johns was created.

The area did deteriorate as it faced urban issues like displacement, neglect, crime, and violence, but by the end of the 1900s and into the 2000s urban renewal efforts began. Renovations, construction, and a new light rail (MAX Yellow Line) brought energy to the area, and revitalized community efforts embraced NoPo's unique offerings.

DIVERSITY IN NOPO

North Portland is the perfect blend of residential neighborhoods, small commercial streets (N Lombard Street, N Mississippi Avenue, and N Williams Avenue), industrial elements (Port of Portland and numerous manufacturing distribution centers), and unbridled nature (Smith and Bybee Wetlands Natural Area, Columbia Slough, and Hayden Island). It is home to the Portland Expo Center, the Portland International Raceway, and the University of Portland as well.

Hosting artists, students, port workers, birdwatchers, race car fans, coffee drinkers, dive bar enthusiasts, and jazz lovers, North Portland is also one of the most ethnically diverse areas in the city. With mass transit connections to downtown and incredible access to nature, this longstanding community continues to expand and develop today.

NOTABLE NOPO NEIGHBORHOODS TO WANDER

These are just some of the NoPo neighborhoods waiting to be explored.

ST. JOHNS Visit Smith and Bybee Wetlands for kayaking, canoeing, and hiking. With coffee shops, restaurants, antique shops, and more on Lombard, St. Johns's independent spirit and small-town feel can be seen at the yearly St. Johns Bizarre and Parade.

CATHEDRAL PARK Cathedral Park's crowning jewel is its namesake park and the stunning St. Johns Bridge. Connecting to Forest Park in Northwest Portland, St. Johns Bridge was built in 1931 and is the only suspension bridge in Portland and the Willamette Valley.

UNIVERSITY PARK Near the University of Portland, University Park may be the perfect place to settle. N Lombard Street provides loads of food choices and its proximity to the river offers stellar views.

N MISSISSIPPI AVENUE Technically in Boise, which straddles North and Northeast Portland, N Mississippi Avenue celebrates mixed cultures and quirkiness in its funky shops, food carts, colorful art, and historic homes.

OVERLOOK Find some of the most spectacular views around! From here you can see Mount Hood, the Willamette with its many bridges, Forest Park, and the downtown skyline. Tree-lined streets, historic homes, and plenty of parks complete this small neighborhood.

HAYDEN ISLAND Surrounded by the Columbia River between the city of Vancouver and Portland sits Hayden Island. It has a variety of offerings, from beaches and nature preserves to loads of houseboats and tax-free shopping.

BUILD BRIDGES—AND DECORATE!

Inspired by St. Johns Bridge and other bridges in Portland, design a new bridge to be built along the Willamette. Use your imagination sprinkled with a little Portland weirdness to come up with something unique and unforgettable. Perhaps your bridge is rose themed with ornate towers covered with roses, or maybe your bridge is a living forest. The options are limitless!

PORTLAND PARKS

Containing over 10,000 acres of public parks and nature areas, Portland is home to one of the largest municipal parks in the United States—Forest Park in North Portland—as well as the smallest—Mill Ends Park in downtown. Whether it's forested, marshlands, manicured, or with playgrounds, the greenspaces and at least 279 parks capture the city's environmentally friendly and outdoorsy vibe!

GOING GREEN

Portland's first parks were acquired in 1852 in downtown from Daniel Lownsdale and William Chapman. As the years passed, the city acquired other parks from family donations as well as consolidated lands. By the turn of the twentieth century as the world exploded with industrialization, Portland decided it needed an actual parks system plan and hired the famous architectural firm Olmsted Brothers. The Olmsteds' plan included not only parks but also incorporated neighborhood designs, scenic parkways, and pedestrian paths throughout the city. Some of the plan was embraced, but many of the land purchases did not occur. Still, the Olmsted Brothers' plan was not for waste. Over the decades, the plan has guided the city's parks development.

Here are some park highlights in Portland not to be missed.

WASHINGTON PARK (SW) Close to the city's core, Washington Park has over 400 acres of wooded areas and many attractions, making it one of the most popular parks in the city.

INTERNATIONAL ROSE TEST GARDEN: Started during World War I for fear that many rose species were being destroyed in Europe, the International Rose Test

Garden began. Fast forward a century and you'll find over 7,000 rose plants there, making up hundreds and hundreds of varieties.

PORTLAND JAPANESE GARDEN: Opened in 1967, this traditional Japanese garden is thought to be one of the best and most authentic in the country. You'll feel as if you've been transported to Japan as you meander past the koi pond, bonsai, and a variety of gardens.

HOYT ARBORETUM: Lace up your shoes and head out on one of the many trails in Hoyt Arboretum to explore thousands of different tree and shrub species from every continent except Antarctica. There are trails for all levels, many providing vantage points to certain plant varieties.

SPOTS IN WASHINGTON PARK FOR YOUNG EXPLORERS

Washington Park is a paradise for the whole family! First, head to the World Forestry Center to learn about forests around the world and how the timber industry has played such a crucial role in Portland and Oregon's history. Next, wander to the Oregon Zoo to see animals of all kinds. And for small ones under age eight, Portland Children's Museum has loads of interactive spaces to discover. There is also the Rose Garden Children's Park with an outdoor playground where the kids can run free!

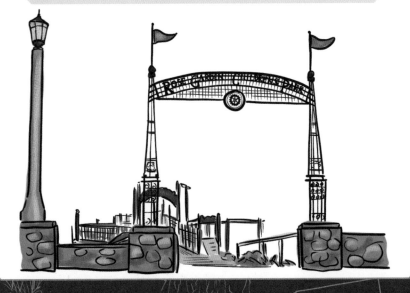

FOREST PARK (NW) Forest Park has over 5,000 acres of forest land and more than 80 miles of trails, home to birds, animals, plants, streams, groves, and a huge variety of trees. In addition to hiking and biking, it also offers a couple unique sites to explore.

PITTOCK MANSION: Arriving in the mid-1800s as a poor man, Henry Pittock worked hard to build a life of community service. He found success in many industries, including developing the city's newspaper, what is now *The Oregonian*. By the 1910s Pittock and his wife, Georgiana, amassed enough wealth to build their 23-room French Renaissance-style mansion on the edge of Forest Park. The Pittock Mansion offers rotating art exhibits and reveals what life was like in early Portland.

WITCH'S CASTLE: What was built in the 1930s as a park ranger station and a public restroom has now become a place of enchantment that people call the Witch's Castle. The now moss-covered stone building is near the 1850s homestead of the Danford Balch's family. After the daughter Anna ignored her father's disapproval and eloped with Mortimer Stump, a man hired to build the Balch home, Balch murdered Stump in cold blood. Balch was later executed for his crime, but people still believe that Stump haunts this site, seeking revenge.

PORTLAND ADULT SOAPBOX DERBY

Every summer on the third Saturday of August, Mount Tabor Park hosts the Portland Adult Soapbox Derby, a wild, wacky event where grownups don their derby cars and race down the extinct volcano. The cars are elaborately decorated, the participants are energetic, and the crowds love every minute of it.

MOUNT TABOR (SE) Not only does Portland have an extinct volcano, but it was also made into a park. Mount Tabor Park rises 630 feet above neighboring areas in the central part of Southeast Portland. The park has plenty of trails (with stairs) as well as three reservoirs. There are also basketball and tennis courts, a picnic area, a dog park, a community garden, a playground, and even a visitor center. Mount Tabor is the perfect place to take a break and soak up the view looking back at the city skyline.

SAUVIE ISLAND

While not technically a park, Sauvie Island is a nature lover's paradise. Only 10 miles from downtown Portland and northwest of NoPo, this rural wonderland is one of the largest islands in the US. Head across St. Johns Bridge, north along Forest Park, and over the quaint Sauvie Island Bridge to get a taste of what Portland felt like when it was just farmlands and forests. Today, Sauvie Island is the perfect place to get away from it all. Go hiking, biking, birdwatching, kayaking, berry picking, fishing, hunting, or just plain relaxing with a book on a beach.

NATURE WALK

Take a nature walk through one or several of the parks Portland offers and use the prompts here to discover the beautiful things you find!

Look closely at a fern and draw one of its curling fronds.

Capture a silhouette of a magnificent pine.

Doodle a troop of mushrooms.

Look on the forest floor and sketch the bugs you see.

Tape in a colorful or oddly shaped leaf here.

Draw a portrait of the most beautiful rose you found.

Race to

Too many doughnuts. Go back 2.

Shoo, moth! It's vintage!

Hidden trails await!

Jump ahead by taking the bridge!

Recycle and go ahead 3.

Take the tram and soar toward the end!

TACOS

Farm Fresh

Menu

START

Ah, the smell of roses!

Can't decide what to eat at the food pod. Go back 1.

78

THE JOURNAL

BEST OF PORTLAND

Fill out the lists below with your favorites from exploring Portland.

BEST SIGHTS

_____
_____
_____
_____
_____
_____
_____
_____
_____
_____

BEST EATS

_____
_____
_____
_____
_____
_____
_____
_____
_____
_____
_____
_____
_____

BEST SHOPPING

_____
_____
_____
_____
_____
_____
_____
_____
_____

BEST DRINKS & NIGHTLIFE

_____
_____
_____
_____
_____
_____
_____
_____
_____
_____
_____

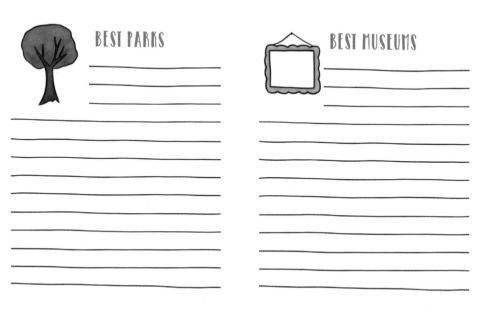

BEST PARKS

_____
_____
_____
_____
_____
_____
_____
_____
_____
_____
_____

BEST MUSEUMS

_____
_____
_____
_____
_____
_____
_____
_____
_____

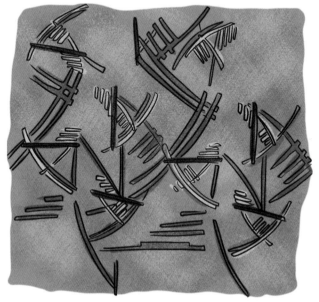

_The infamous and trendy pattern from the carpet
at Portland International Airport._

DAY

#____

DATE _____

RATING ☆☆☆☆☆

WEATHER

PLACES VISITED

_____
_____
_____
_____
_____
_____
_____
_____
_____
_____

BEST EATS OF THE DAY

_____
_____
_____
_____
_____
_____
_____
_____

QUOTE OF THE DAY

_____
_____
_____
_____

ONLY IN PORTLAND

_____
_____
_____
_____

SOMETHING I SAW TODAY

DAY

#____

DATE _____

RATING ☆☆☆☆☆

WEATHER

PLACES VISITED

_____
_____
_____
_____
_____
_____
_____
_____

BEST EATS OF THE DAY

_____
_____
_____
_____
_____
_____
_____

QUOTE OF THE DAY

_____
_____
_____
_____

ONLY IN PORTLAND

_____
_____
_____

SOMETHING I SAW TODAY

DAY #____

DATE _____ RATING ☆☆☆☆☆

WEATHER

PLACES VISITED

_____
_____
_____
_____
_____
_____
_____
_____
_____
_____

BEST EATS OF THE DAY

_____
_____
_____
_____
_____
_____
_____
_____

QUOTE OF THE DAY

_____
_____
_____
_____

ONLY IN PORTLAND

_____
_____
_____
_____

SOMETHING I SAW TODAY

DAY

#____

DATE _____   RATING ☆☆☆☆☆

WEATHER ☀ ⛅ ☁ ☂ 🧢

PLACES VISITED

_____
_____
_____
_____
_____
_____
_____
_____
_____

BEST EATS OF THE DAY

_____
_____
_____
_____
_____
_____
_____

QUOTE OF THE DAY

_____
_____
_____
_____

ONLY IN PORTLAND

_____
_____
_____

SOMETHING I SAW TODAY

DAY

#____

DATE _____

RATING ☆☆☆☆☆

WEATHER

PLACES VISITED

_____
_____
_____
_____
_____
_____
_____
_____

BEST EATS OF THE DAY

_____
_____
_____
_____
_____

QUOTE OF THE DAY

_____
_____
_____

ONLY IN PORTLAND

_____
_____
_____

SOMETHING I SAW TODAY

DAY

#____

DATE _____   RATING ☆☆☆☆☆

WEATHER

PLACES VISITED

_____
_____
_____
_____
_____
_____
_____
_____
_____

BEST EATS OF THE DAY

_____
_____
_____
_____
_____
_____
_____

QUOTE OF THE DAY

_____
_____
_____
_____

ONLY HERE
ADVENTURE & FUN THINGS

ONLY IN PORTLAND

_____
_____
_____

SOMETHING I SAW TODAY

DAY

#____

DATE _____

RATING ☆☆☆☆☆

WEATHER

PLACES VISITED

_____
_____
_____
_____
_____
_____
_____
_____
_____

BEST EATS OF THE DAY

_____
_____
_____
_____
_____
_____
_____

QUOTE OF THE DAY

_____
_____
_____
_____

ONLY IN PORTLAND

_____
_____
_____

SOMETHING I SAW TODAY

BREWERY BLOCKS

The five-block Brewery Blocks traces back to 1864,
when Henry Weinhard purchased an area from George
Bottler's City Brewery to expand his beer-making business.
Within seven years his lager became famous throughout the Pacific
Northwest and California, and was even sold to China, the Philippines,
and Japan. Weinhard's brewery withstood many changes over the decades,
from producing near-beer (which had less alcohol), syrups, and sodas to
obey Prohibition rules, to merging with Arnold Blitz of Portland Brewing to
become the Blitz-Weinhard Company. But in August of 1999, its last beer
was brewed in Portland and the whole operation moved to Washington.
Luckily, the historic buildings were preserved, and today
Henry's Tavern stands as a homage to Weinhard
and Portland's beer lovers.

The "Noble Architect," by Ruth Greenberg and Dave Laubenthal, is at NE Alberta Street and NE 18th Avenue.

BURNSIDE SKATEPARK

In October 1990, a group of
skateboarders decided to embellish an area
below the Burnside Bridge in Central Eastside
for better skating. With just a few cement bags,
they poured some ramps—and the legendary Burnside
Skatepark was born! As more ramps and additions
were added and continual improvements were
made, the skate park eventually grew
to its celebrity status.

The Burnside Skatepark
is at SE 2nd Avenue.

St. Johns Bridge is at
8600 NW Bridge Avenue.

The Gold Medal Garden is at the International Rose Test Garden at 400 SW Kingston Avenue.

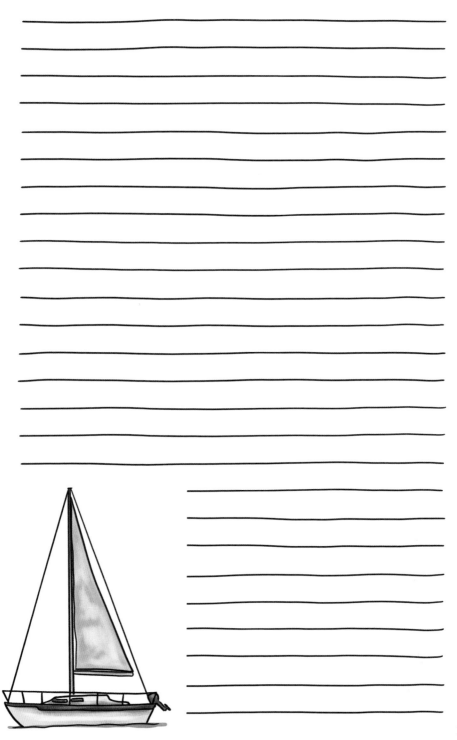

WORLD NAKED BIKE RIDE

What started as a protest to our society's dependence on oil has grown into an annual tradition that not only celebrates cycling, but also allows people to share their viewpoints as well as embrace body positivity. This event is yet another example of Portland's activist culture and reveals the liberal community spirit in action!

SE Portland

OMSI

PORTLAND
JAPANESE
GARDEN

611 SW Kingston Avenue

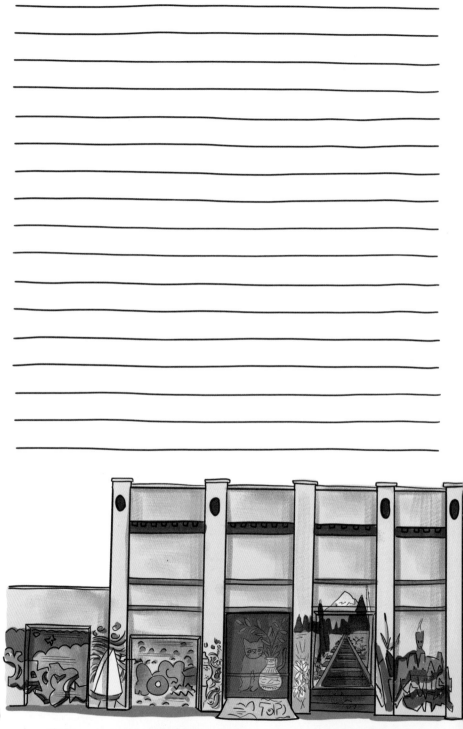

STREET ART

With all the craftspeople, artists, and makers in Portland, naturally the city is filled with street art. Thanks in part to Portland Street Art Alliance and many business owners, a new initiative called Viaduct Arts was formed to decorate as many walls and spaces throughout the Central Eastside neighborhood. The goal is to provide free access to art for the entire community and promote various identities that give uniqueness to CEID. If you see them, snap a shot of these colorful spots that brighten even the grayest of Portland days.

DEDICATION

To Nico, one of the most agreeable travelers and happy souls I know. I am so very lucky to have you as a son. Your easygoing style, honesty, and empathy mixed with silliness, creativity, and a hint of sarcasm make our adventures together one of a kind. From seeking out every single unique bread option a country may offer to discovering new ways to photograph animals on safari, I love you from the bottom of my heart.

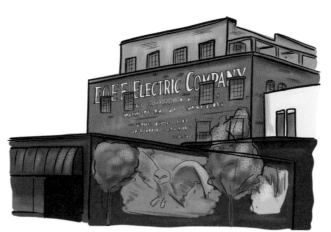

Built in 1905, the Eoff Electric Company headquarters is the first building in the Pearl to be renovated into condos. Now known as City Lofts, the building is at 1011 NW Glisan Street.

Text and Illustrations © 2022 by Betsy Beier

Published by West Margin Press®

WEST MARGIN PRESS

WestMarginPress.com

LCCN: 2021949726

ISBN: 9781513289427

Proudly distributed by
Ingram Publisher Services

Printed in China
1 2 3 4 5

WEST MARGIN PRESS
Publishing Director: Jennifer Newens
Marketing Manager: Alice Wertheimer
Project Specialist: Micaela Clark
Editor: Olivia Ngai
Design & Production: Rachel Lopez Metzger